BUILDING BLOCKS OF BIOLOGY

ORGANS AND ORGAN SYSTEMS

Written by Alex Woolf

Illustrated by Ruth Bennett

www.worldbook.com

Co-published by agreement between Shi Tu Hui and World Book, Inc.

Shi Tu Hui
Room 1807, Block 1,
#3 West Dawang Road
Chaoyang District, Beijing 100025
P.R. China

World Book, Inc.
180 North LaSalle Street
Suite 900
Chicago, Illinois 60601
USA

© 2026. All rights reserved. This volume may not be reproduced in whole or in part in any form without prior written permission from the publisher.

WORLD BOOK and the GLOBE DEVICE are registered trademarks or trademarks of World Book, Inc.

Library of Congress Control Number: 2025942739

Building Blocks of Biology
ISBN: 978-0-7166-6737-7 (set, hard cover)

Organs and Organ Systems
ISBN: 978-0-7166-6740-7 (hard cover)

Also available as:
ISBN: 978-0-7166-6760-5 (e-book)
ISBN: 978-0-7166-6750-6 (soft cover)

WORLD BOOK STAFF

Editorial

Vice President
Tom Evans

Senior Manager, New Content
Jeff De La Rosa

Proofreader
Nathalie Strassheim

Graphics and Design

Senior Visual Communications Designer
Melanie Bender

Acknowledgments
Writer: Alex Woolf
Illustrator: Ruth Bennett/The Bright Agency

TABLE OF CONTENTS

World's Smallest Vehicle 4

Digestive System 8

Circulatory System 14

Respiratory System 20

Science Fun with Fur:
Measure Your Lung Capacity 24

Nervous System 26

Back Home 32

Life on the Edge: Bioprinting Organs 34

Show What You Know 38

Answers and Words to Know 40

There is a glossary on page 40. Terms defined in the glossary are in type **that looks like this** on their first appearance.

Do you know what the prefix *nano-* means?
See page 40 for the answer.

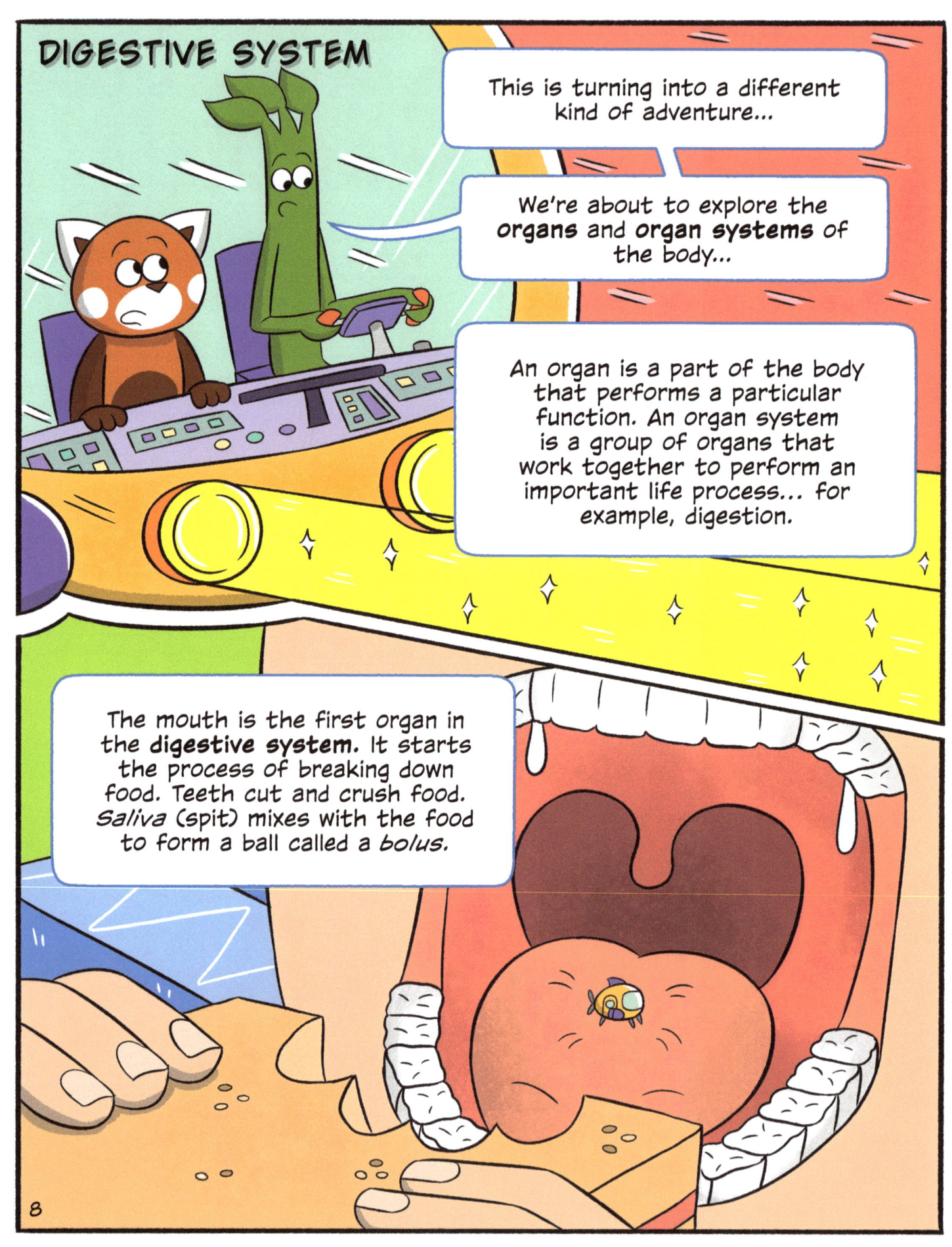

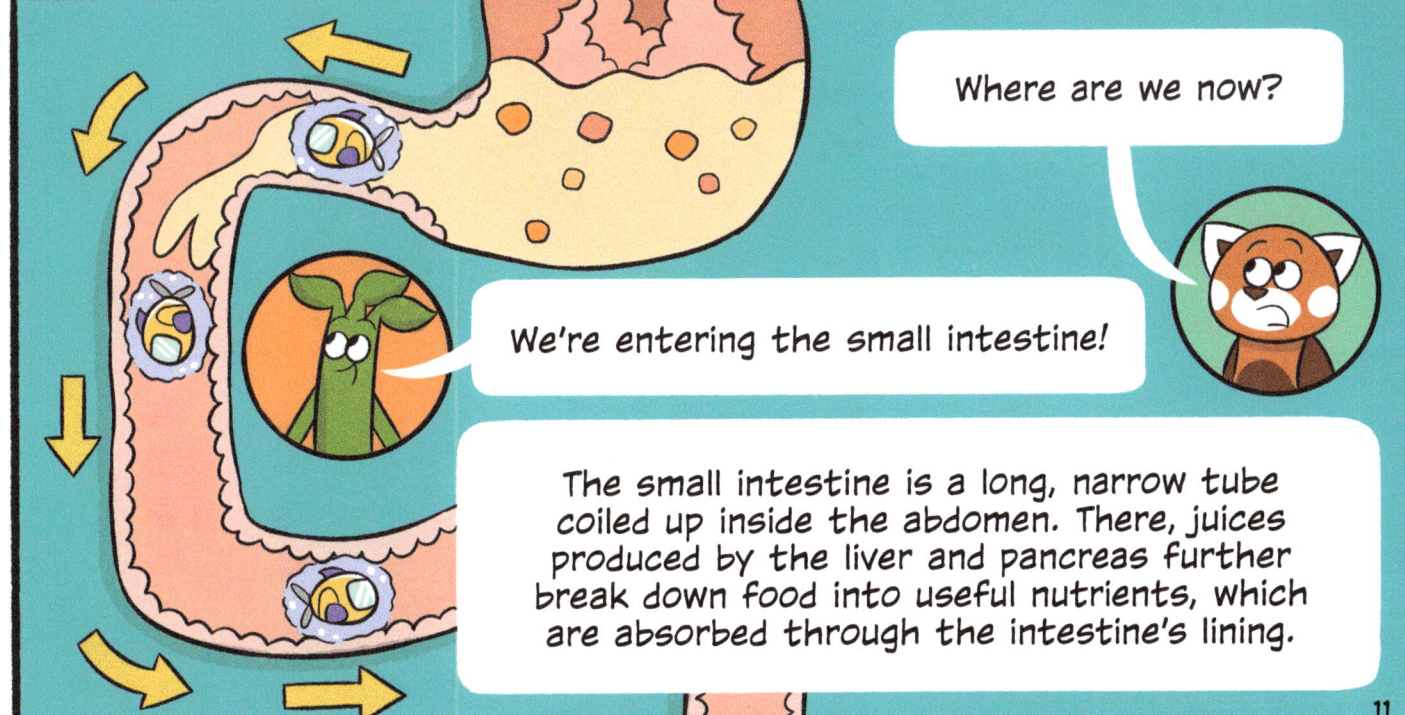

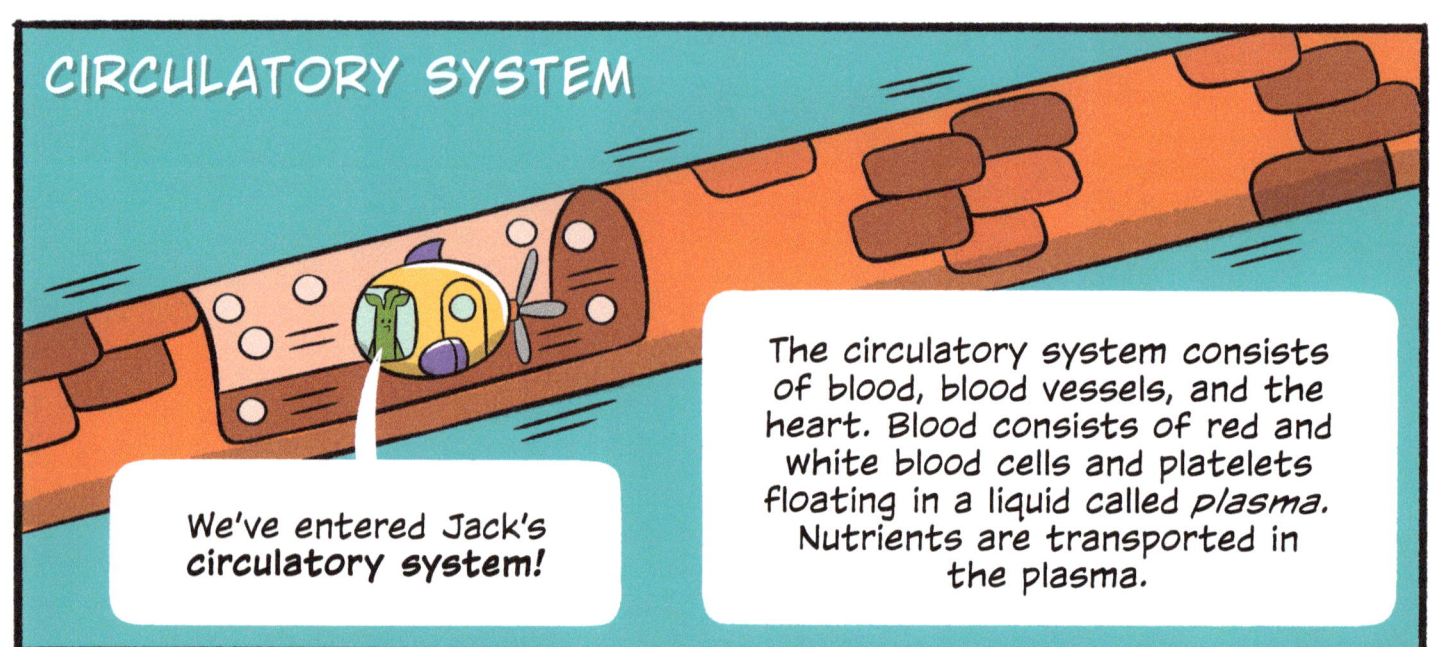

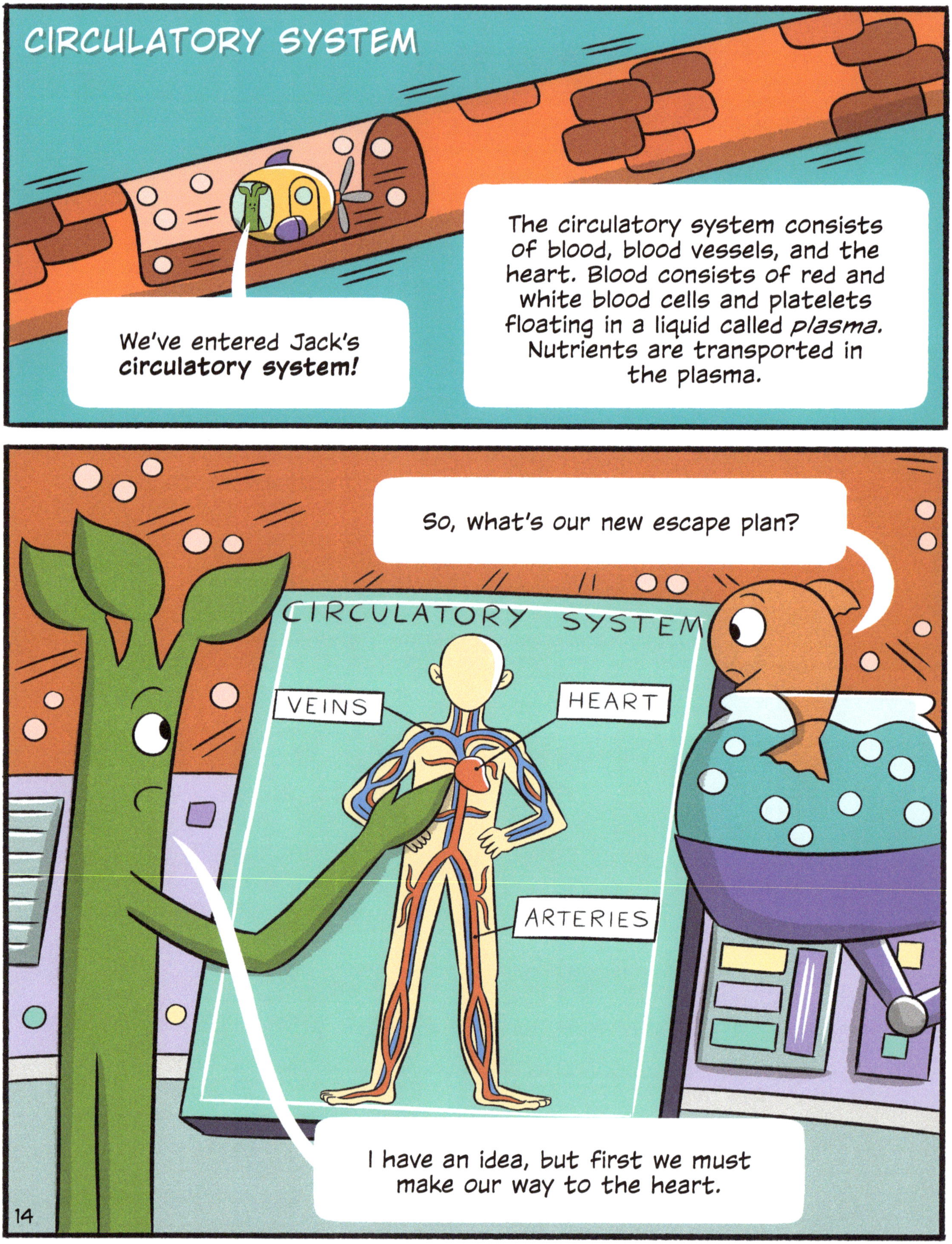

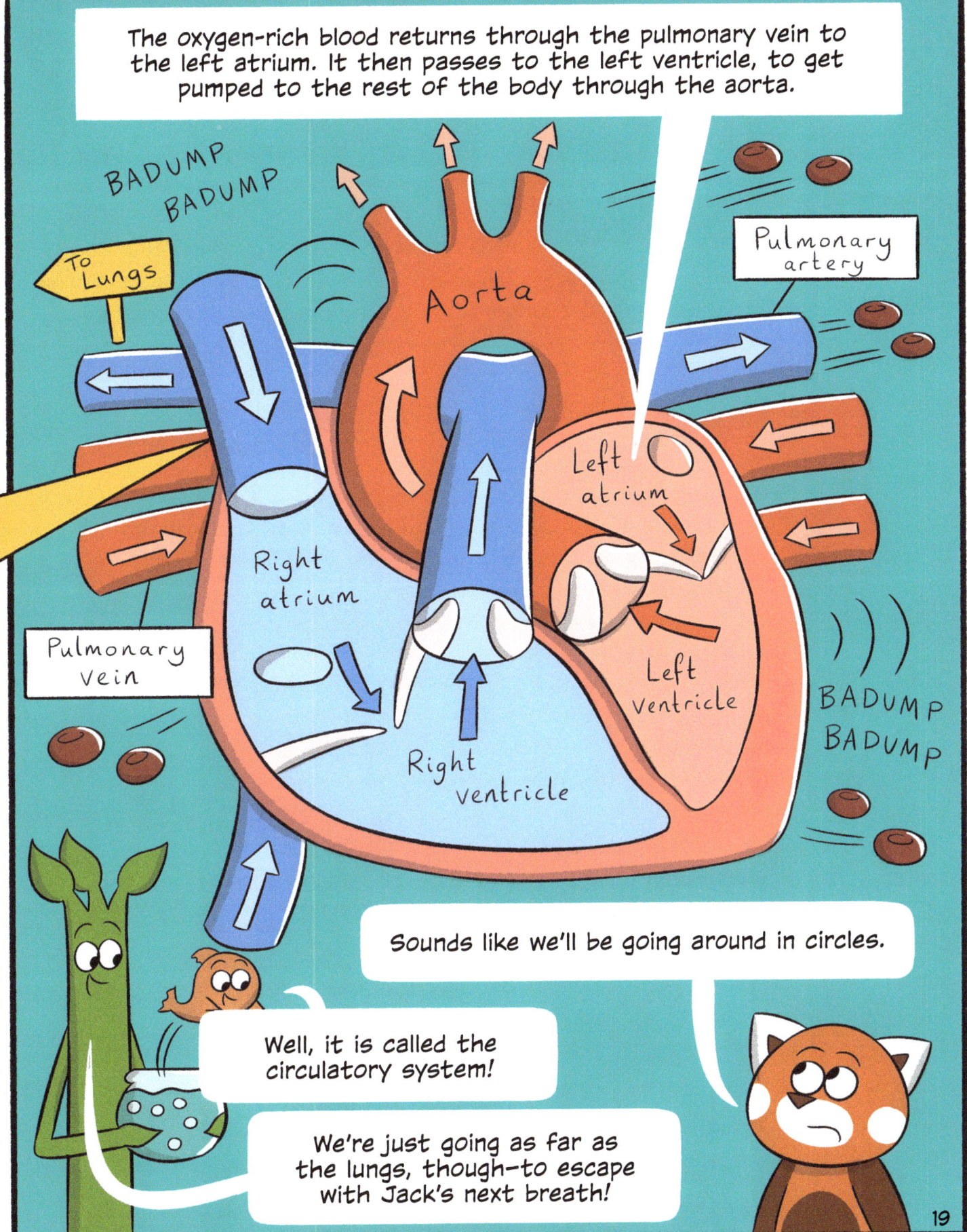

RESPIRATORY SYSTEM

The Nanoship hurtles through the heart and along the pulmonary artery.

It enters a network of capillaries, and finally reaches the lungs.

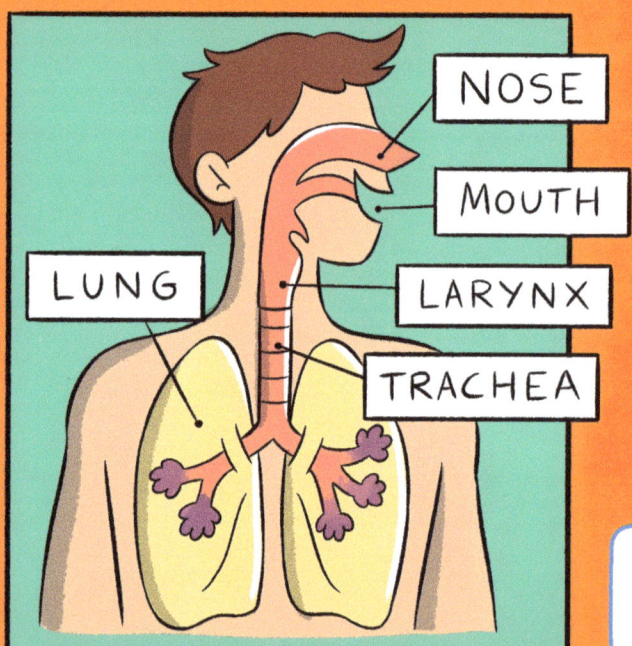

The **respiratory system** includes the mouth, nose, throat, larynx, trachea, and lungs. This system brings in oxygen, which the cells of the body need to unlock energy from food. It also gets rid of carbon dioxide, a waste gas.

What's that lumpy thing that keeps getting bigger and smaller?

That's an **alveolus**—one of many air sacs in Jack's lungs.

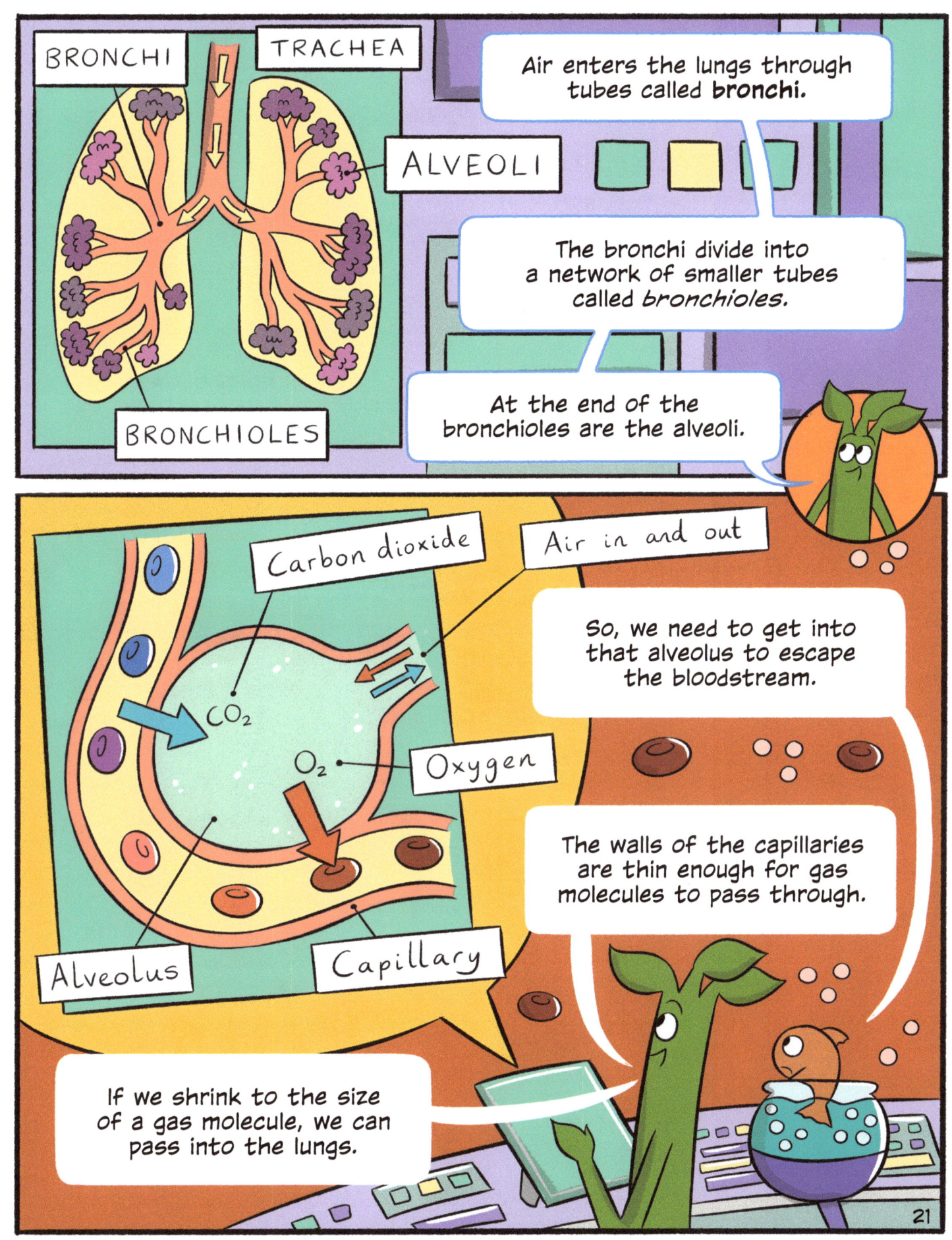

① Carefully place the bottle upside down in the bowl of water and take the cap off, being careful not to spill any water.

② Put one end of the straw or tube inside the bottle.

③ Take a deep breath and breathe into the bottle. Your breath will push the water out.

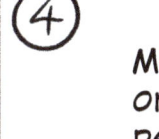

④ Mark the level of water on the bottle with the permanent marker. This shows you how much air your lungs can hold.

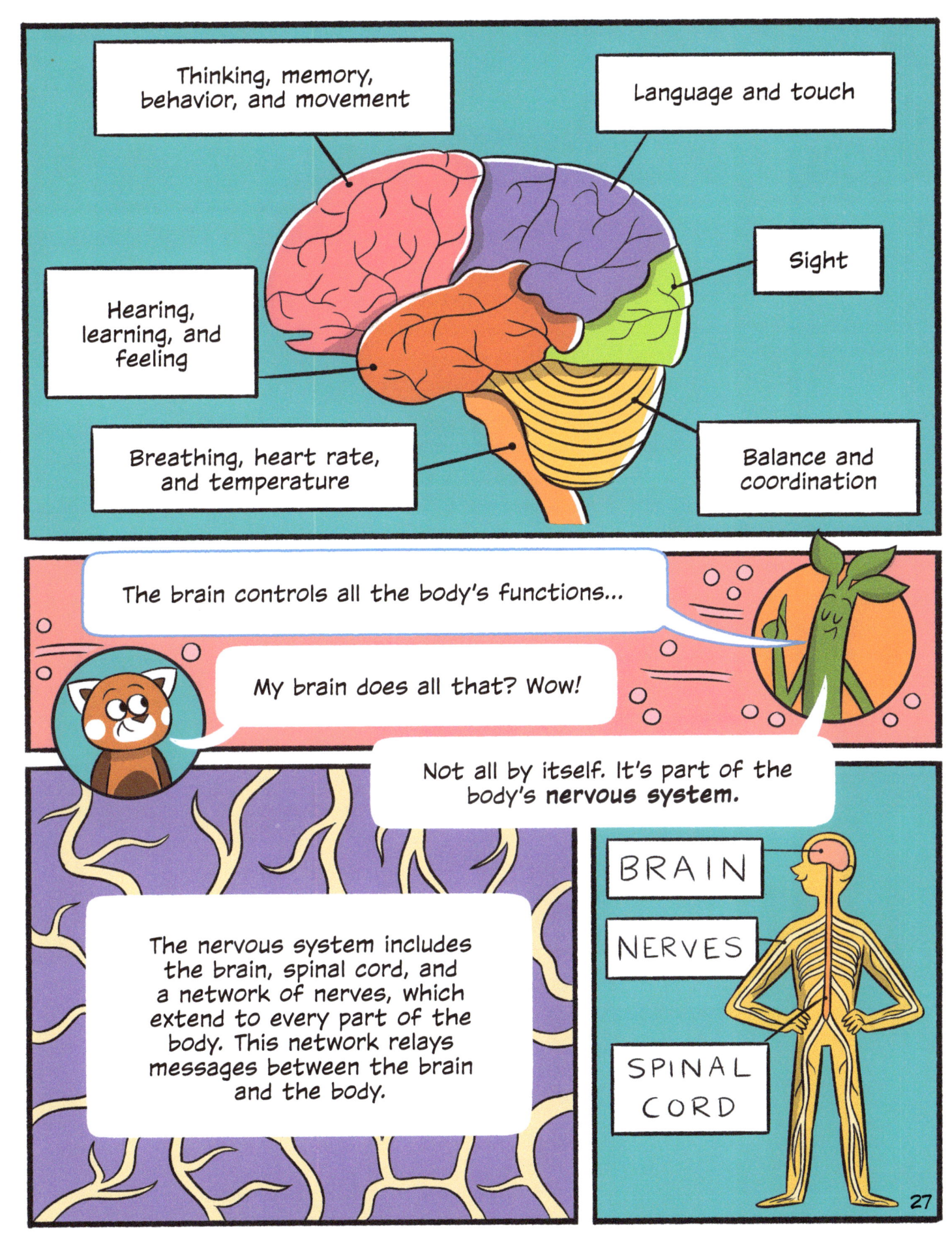

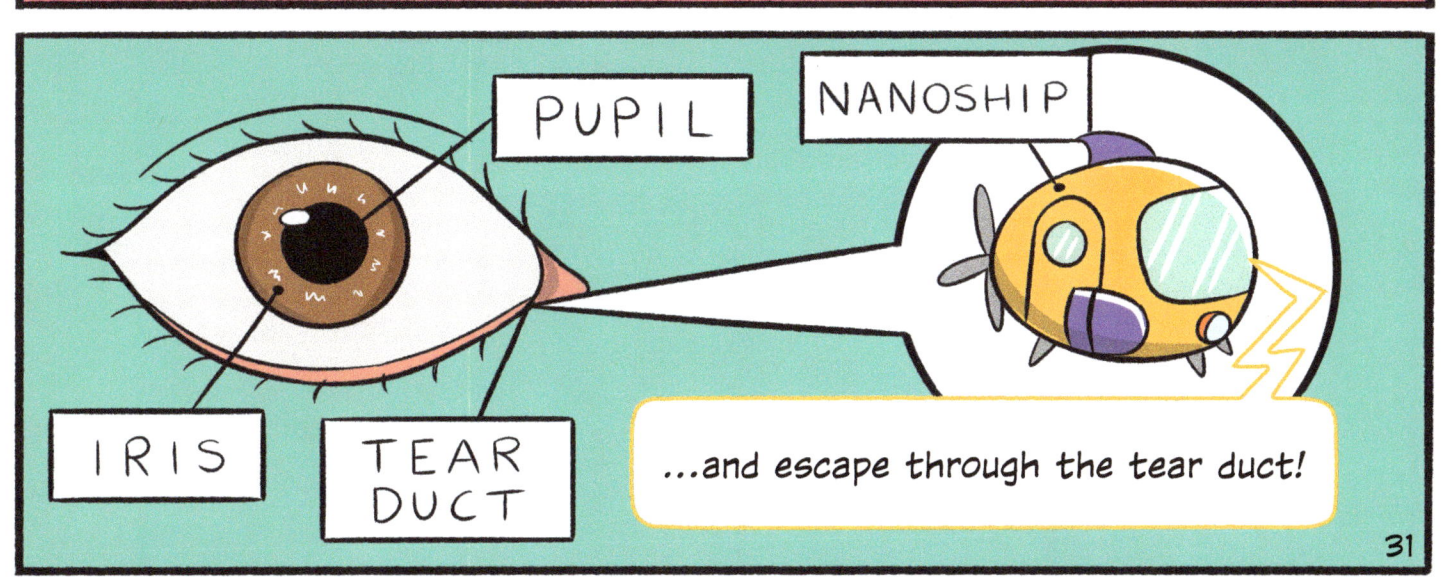

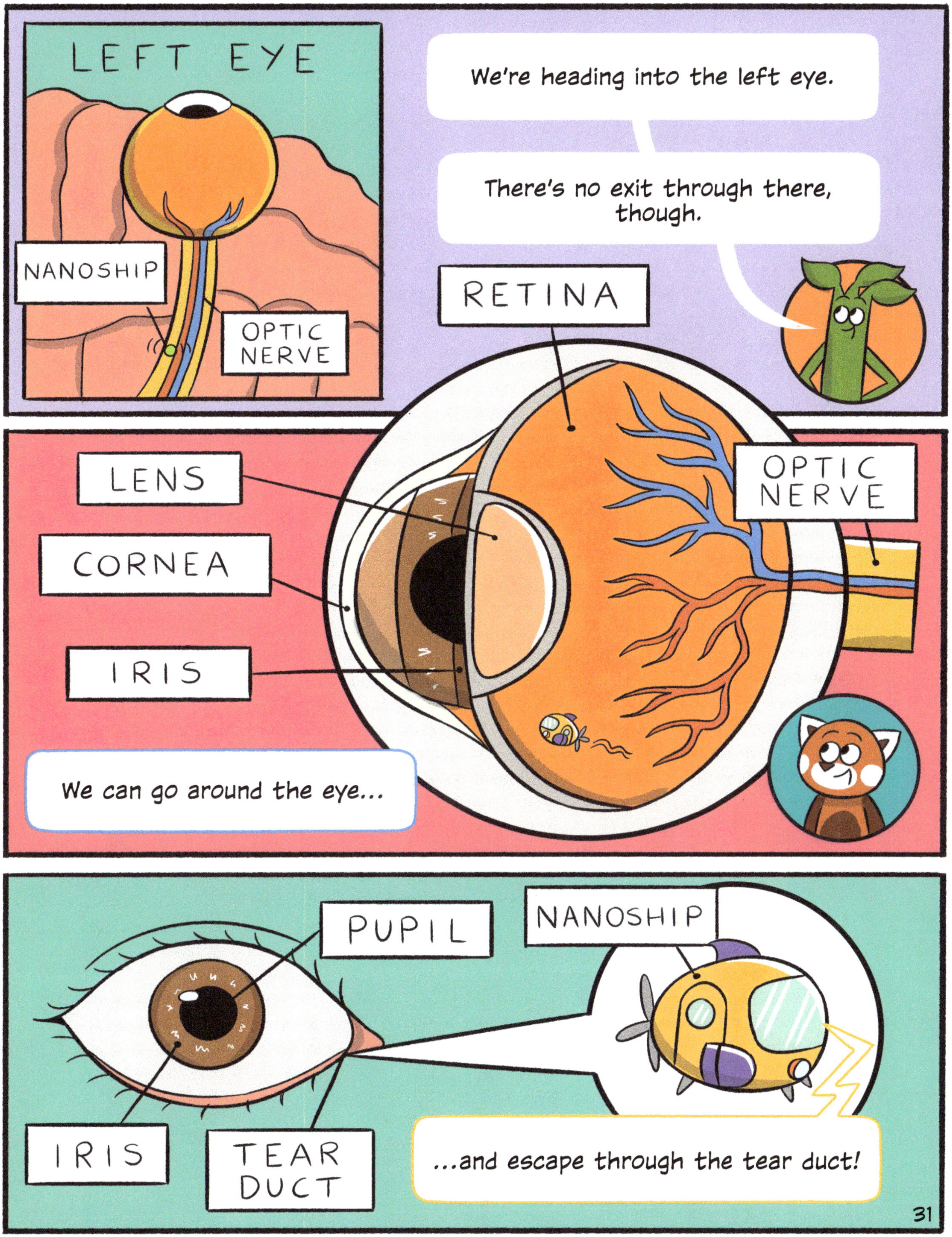

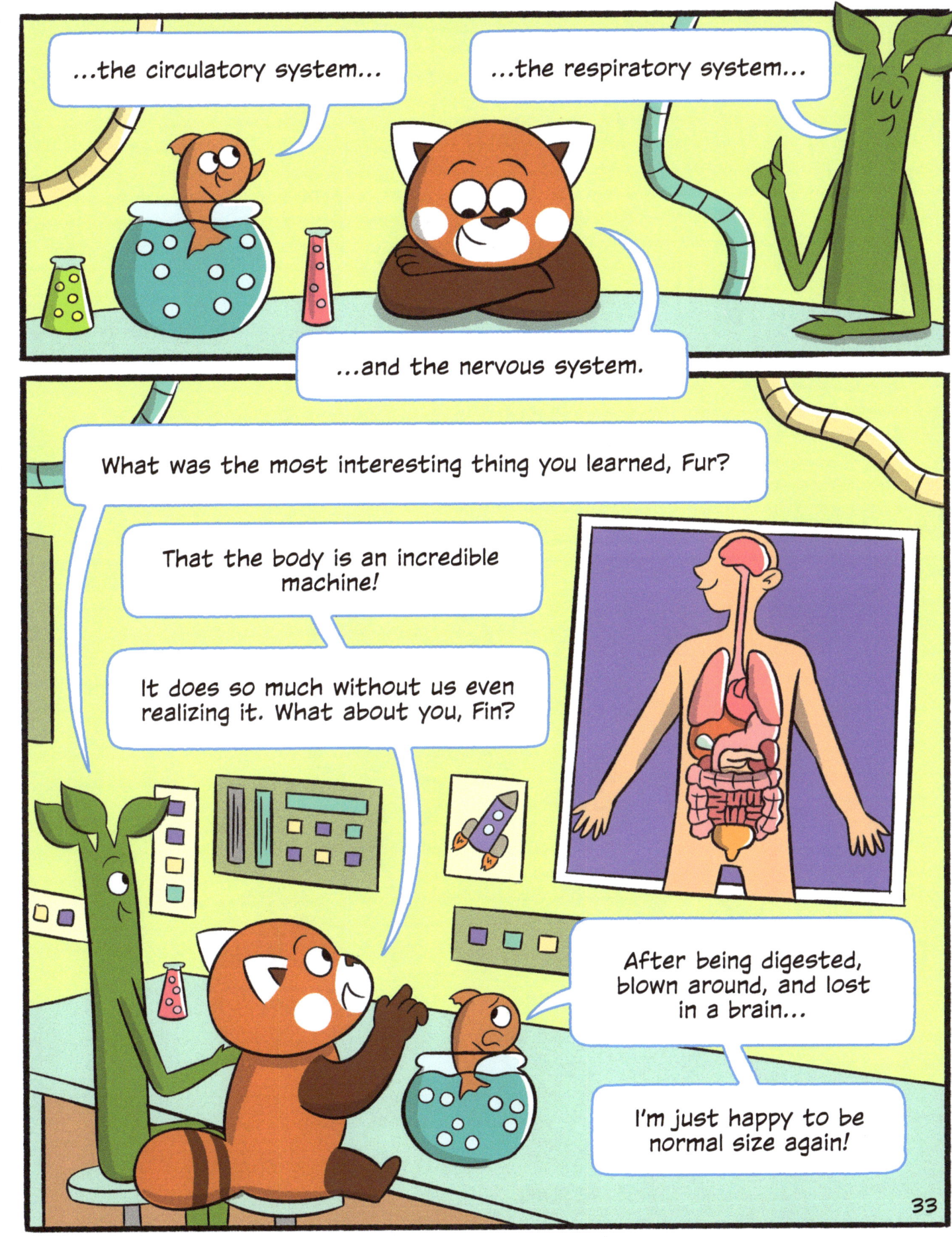

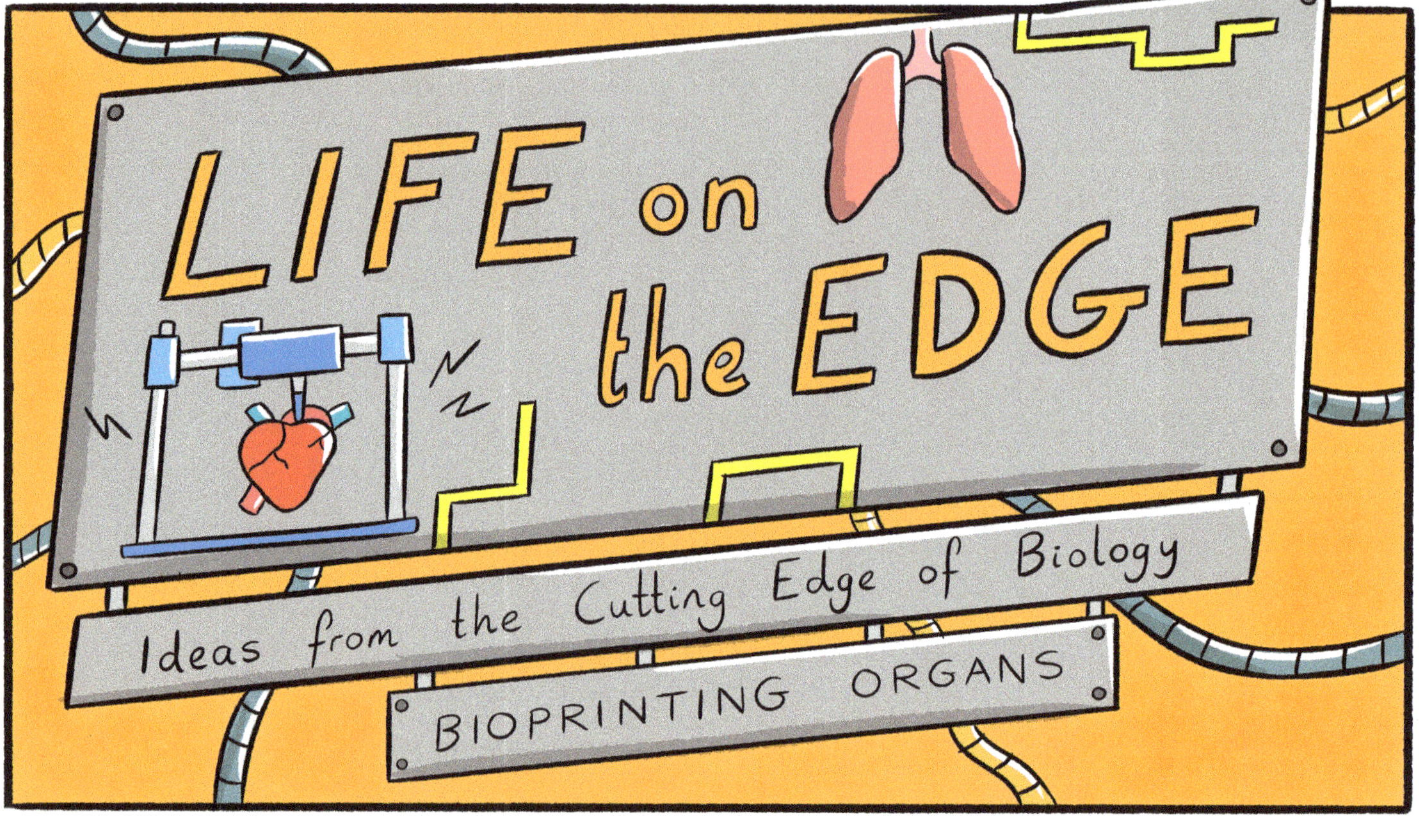

LIFE on the EDGE

Ideas from the Cutting Edge of Biology

BIOPRINTING ORGANS

A week later...

"I can't stop thinking about our trip. The organs are so cool!"

"They certainly are! In fact, I'd love to try making one myself."

"Why would you do that?"

"Organs are highly complex structures...

Today, we can only **bioprint** simple structures, such as skin patches, blood vessels, and cartilage...

Buzzzzzzzzzz

In the future, we might be able to bioprint hearts and lungs!

Neat!

BUZZZZZZZZZZZ

37

SHOW WHAT YOU KNOW

1. Name the organ system that performs each of these functions:

   A. brings oxygen into the body
   B. relays messages between the brain and the body
   C. breaks down food into nutrients
   D. delivers oxygen and nutrients to the body's cells

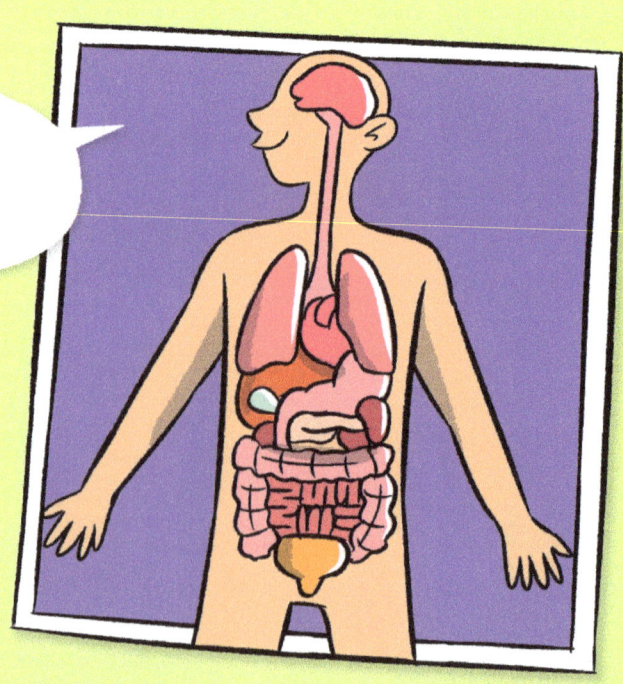

2. To which organ system does each of the following belong?

   A. spinal cord
   B. stomach
   C. lungs
   D. veins
   E. small intestine

3. Choose the right word.

A. (Sensory/Motor) neurons carry messages from the brain telling the muscles to move.

B. (Arteries/Veins) carry oxygen-rich blood from the heart to the rest of the body.

C. The process of digestion begins in the (mouth/stomach).

4. Match each word to its description.

alveoli
bolus
caplliaries
villi

A. fingerlike projections that help absorb food in the small intestine

B. a ball of saliva and chewed up food

C. tiny vessels that connect veins and arteries

D. air sacs in the lungs

See page 40 for answers.

ANSWERS

page 7: The prefix *nano-* means billionth. Nanotechnology—such as the nanoship—is designed to operate at scales around one-billionth of a meter, or 0.000000001 meter. That's tiny!

page 13: esophagus; small intestine

page 17: Red blood cells carry oxygen around the body. White blood cells attack germs.

page 29: brain, spinal cord, and nerves

SHOW WHAT YOU KNOW ANSWERS
pages 38-39:

1. A. respiratory system
   B. nervous system
   C. digestive system
   D. circulatory system

2. A. nervous system
   B. digestive system
   C. respiratory system
   D. circulatory system
   E. digestive system

3. A. motor
   B. arteries
   C. mouth

4. A. villi
   B. bolus
   C. capillaries
   D. alveoli

WORDS TO KNOW

alveolus (plural, alveoli) tiny air sacs in the lungs that enable oxygen to enter the bloodstream.

bioprinting 3D printing using materials that contain living cells.

bronchi tubes through which air enters the lungs.

capillaries tiny blood vessels that connect arteries and veins.

circulatory system the organ system that transports oxygen and nutrients throughout the body.

digestive system the organ system that breaks down food to produce energy.

esophagus a tube that connects the mouth to the stomach.

organ a part of the body that performs a particular function.

organ system a group of organs that work together to fulfill an important life process.

nervous system the organ system that carries messages between the brain and the rest of the body.

respiratory system the organ system that brings oxygen into the body and gets rid of carbon dioxide.

villi fingerlike projections in the small intestine that help to absorb nutrients from food.

www.ingramcontent.com/pod-product-compliance
Lightning Source LLC
Chambersburg PA
CBHW061256170426
43191CB00041B/2436